GUARDED BY *God*

In the Midst of an Earthquake!

Samuel Beachy

GUARDED BY *God*

In the Midst of an Earthquake!

Samuel Beachy

Ridgeway Publishing
Medina, New York

GUARDED BY GOD

To order additional copies,
please visit your local
bookstore or contact:

Ridgeway Publishing
3129 Fruit Avenue
Medina, NY 14103
(585) 798-0050 ph.

Printed by:
Ridgeway Publishing

Cover design:
M. Gagarin Design

Printed in the United States of America

ISBN# 978-0-9840985-0-7

Acknowledgments

Primarily, I want to thank God for His protection to us while we were in Costa Rica. Secondly, I want to thank the Lord for giving me wisdom and strength to write this book. Without the Lord's help, this writing project would have been a failure.

I want to thank my six traveling companions for their input from the earthquake experience. Also thanks to Duane and Ruth Nisly for allowing me to glean thoughts from their writings. I want to thank Paul Weaver for allow me to glean thoughts from his letters, which he sent to our families and friends at home. A special thanks to Gracia Schlabach for editing the manuscript.

I want to thank Junior Troyer, Andre Weaver, Herb Miller, Ruben and Marvin Dueck for giving me permission to use their pictures.

We want to thank each one who prayed for us through our earthquake experience. We definitely felt the prayers of the saints.

Introduction

January 8, 2009 began as a day of sightseeing for our group of seven. We gave little thought that the experiences of this day would make vivid, life-long impressions. Before we left for Costa Rica, Junior and Jeremy both felt in their hearts that something unusual was going to happen on this trip. Perhaps God was preparing them for this earthquake experience.

On this Thursday, in the mountains of Costa Rica, the seven of us were reminded in a dramatic way that there is no promise for tomorrow. Life is short. The earth is unstable. Solid ground can slide to the gully below, without a warning. We can be headed for eternity in an instant.

My desire is that this account will glorify God and the great power He demonstrated. It is only because of God's divine protection that the seven of us are still alive and I am able to share this story with others. I shudder to think what could have happened to us. We stared directly at eternity.

I have tried to portray the story accurately but my mind could not find words to describe it all. As I wrote, I couldn't help but relive the terror and disbelief followed by uncertainty and confusion. At times my emotions almost overwhelmed me. I could hardly go on. Yet I felt the Lord beckoning me to continue writing about His power and goodness.

Table of Contents

Costa Rica, Central America

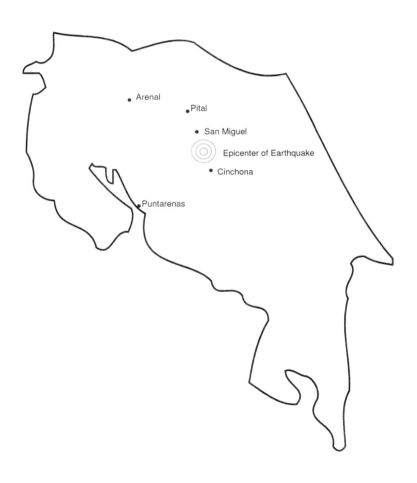

- Arenal
- Pital
- San Miguel
- Epicenter of Earthquake
- Cinchona
- Puntarenas

Chapter One

Cost Rica Bound

After months of planning, January 7, 2009 finally arrived. Excitement was high! Six energetic fellows from Ohio would step on a jetliner and fly south to Central America. Here they would meet a friend from Tennessee and begin their travels through tropical Costa Rica.

The passengers of the expedition consisted of seven single boys. There were three brothers, Jeremy, Andre, and Jon Anthony Weaver, and three other fellows, Junior Troyer, Leroy Yutzy, and Lewis Stutzman, all from Georgetown, Ohio. At that time, I (Samuel Beachy) lived at Belvidere, Tennessee. In April, 2009 my family moved to an new outreach community at Fredonia, Kentucky.

Each one of our group has their own unique

character, shape, and size. We anticipated an enjoyable time together. I would renew some friendships from Bible school. Junior also expected to enjoy this trip to its fullest. This would possibly be one of the last trips he would take with two of his friends, since Lewis was planning to be married in April and Jeremy was dating. This would be a once-in-a-lifetime experience, traveling together out of the country.

We looked forward to the fulfillment of our plans. If the colorful sights of Costa Rica looked like they did in travel literature, we would see lots of beautiful scenery. Our plans included some vacation time, but the highlight would be to visit missionaries and experience a different climate and culture.

Our itinerary had been carefully planned. We were filled with eager anticipation! (None of us dreamed how drastically the Lord would rearrange our plans.) We would arrive in San Jose on Wednesday, January 7. On Thursday we would drive north toward Arenal, sightseeing along the way. At Arenal we had motel reservations for two nights and would spend some time exploring the parks in that area. Next we would go the brethren near San Carlos. They had a work project lined up for Saturday. Sunday we would worship with them.

On Monday we would head south to the warm Pacific coast and spend a few days at Puntarenas. Next we would drive to Nicaragua, spending the weekend at Waslala. Finally we would return to Managua on Monday for our homeward flight.

My travels in Central America would begin two weeks earlier already. On December 19, 2008, I planned fly to Belize to visit my brother Philip who was teaching school in Cayo. I would meet the other six boys in San Jose. I considered it a rare privilege that it worked out to join my friends on their trip to Costa Rica.

Early Wednesday morning, January 7, the six boys from Ohio boarded their flight. They flew into San Jose, then got the rental vehicle and settled in at a motel. Meanwhile, also on Wednesday morning, I said good-bye to my brother Philip, at the Cayo mission and took the bus to Belize City, a three hour ride. From Belize City I had an afternoon flight to Miami, Florida, then from Miami to San Jose, Costa Rica. Finally, at 10:30 p.m., I stepped off the plane at San Jose. This had been a long, hard day for me because I needed to go through customs twice. Junior and Lewis met me at the airport. It was midnight when we arrived at the motel. I was exhausted and ready for a good night of sleep.

The next morning at six o'clock the alarm clock jangled noisily. Ah, wouldn't a few more winks feel good?

"Let's be off before too late!" said Jeremy. He knew that by mid forenoon misty, gray clouds often rolled in and covered the mountain scenery at higher elevations.

Junior reminded us that we didn't want to let our devotional life slip while we were on vacation. We realized that this is the day that the Lord had made. We would rejoice and be glad in it. We chose "Let My Life Be a Light" for a daily theme song. Our prayer was that we could be a witness as we met people on this trip.

After eating breakfast at the motel, we quickly headed out to our rental vehicle, a white Toyota SUV. To fit seven people and five hundred pounds of luggage into an eight-passenger vehicle was quite a challenge. Finally we strapped some of the luggage up on the luggage rack. The workers at the motel must have chuckled at these Americans with their great volumes of luggage.

At 8:15 we were off. First we drove north toward Poás, the semi-active volcano. We looked forward to great views of the beautiful Central valley from the top of Poás. Sometimes tourists were fortunate enough to see steam geysers within the huge crater. If not, we could at least see the deep, moonscape type hole. Hopefully we could get there before clouds covered the peak.

The skies became more and more overcast as we neared the mountain. Finally we were driving through fine, drizzly rain. When we arrived at the entrance of Volcán Poás National Park, the agent at the ticket booth shook his head. "Do not waste money for a pass."

We looked at each other. Should we take his advice? If we kept going, we would only see more gray clouds. The crater would not be visible.

"I guess we better turn around," Jeremy said, with a hint of disappointment in his voice.

The rest of us agreed. There were other places to see. Maybe it wasn't so cloudy at lower elevations.

From Poás we drove toward Vara Blanca. We encountered many horseshoe curves along the way. Some of the curves on that road are so tight that a straight truck cannot make the turn without backing up and turning more sharply.

As we traveled through the mountain highlands, we soaked in the gorgeous scenery and pleasant temperatures.

"It's hard to imagine that back home in Brown County, Ohio, they're having snow and ice!" exclaimed Jon Anthony. "Here we are enjoying seventy degree weather."

Chapter Two

The La Paz Waterfalls Gardens

At 10:30 we came to La Paz Waterfall Gardens, a private wildlife refuge with a restaurant and lodge. The La Paz River runs directly through the Gardens and tumbles over five waterfalls. It looked like a fairly pricey place, so first Jeremy and Junior went in to check out the entrance cost.

Junior came out with a look of disbelief on his face. "Thirty-five dollars for a ticket! Do we want to spend that much?"

Jeremy knew from an earlier visit to this place that it would be worthwhile to pay for the ticket, but he understood the others' reluctance. "If we keep driving, we'll be able to get a good view of the lowest falls from the road."

That sounded like a good idea and was certainly cheaper than paying thirty-five dollars! We headed back out to the road and drove slowly downhill. At the yellow metal grid bridge we stopped. These falls were lovely, surrounded with lush greenery. Apparently this bridge was a common stopping place for tourists, because a number of small trinket shops were just across the road.

"I'm going across the road to buy some souvenirs," I announced. When I returned a few minutes later, the other fellows were all excited.

"We're ready to go back up to the park reception building and pay for a ticket. It'll be worth it," Junior said.

It sure was worth every cent. As soon as we started down the trails we knew it had been a good decision. First we entered the screened-in aviary, which was a birder's paradise. Here we met a friendly, talkative couple in their upper 60's. They were from England. This couple took a keen interest in the birds. For the next thirty minutes, they joined us boys as we ambled along on the paths.

La Paz Waterfall Gardens Reception Building

The brilliant parrots and toucans had eye catching colors, but at one point our attention was directed to a small brownish bird perched high in a tree.

Junior studied it with his binoculars. "I think it's a Tennessee warbler."

"No, no," said the woman from England slowly.

The man from England also shook his head. "I think it is some other warbler," he said in his careful British accent.

Shrugging his shoulders, Junior gave them a good natured grin. That bird *did* look like the Tennessee warblers he often saw in Ohio.

After leaving the birdhouse we walked down to the butterfly observatory where more than twenty different kinds of butterflies were flitting around. Next we entered the Serpentarium where thirty kinds of reptiles were housed. Our eyes could hardly absorb the bright tropical colors, but there were still more things to see in the frog house and hummingbird garden.

Finally we came to the monkey house. We watched their playful antics with amusement. The agile spider monkeys swung and jumped around in their pen. One monkey seemed unusually restless and was desperately trying to chew through the wire on its pen.

This monkey sensed the impending danger.

"Why is that monkey acting that way?" wondered Lewis.

The rest of us were puzzled, too. There was no obvious reason for its distress.

After observing all the

15.

animals, we continued down the steps that lead to the river. Signs everywhere reminded tourists like us to stay on the trails. Considering the steep ravine, it would have quite risky to leave the trails.

The trail ran along the river for nearly a mile, with lots of steps and two foot bridges. We could feel the spray from the five waterfalls as we walked right above, below and next to them. The highest falls dropped 120 feet. The views were breathtaking.

The river trail ended at a gift shop and shuttle bus pickup. We spent a few minutes looking at souvenirs. I picked out some postcards, then noticed that the green shuttle bus was waiting.

"I better pay for these right now or I'll miss my ride." I thought.

I looked around for a cashier, but no one was around. I considered putting the postcards back, but finally I saw a gentleman coming. I quickly paid for my purchase and arrived at the bus before all the people were loaded. The green shuttle bus took us back up to the parking lot.

We piled into our vehicle, with Lewis taking the driver's seat. Now we were ready for our drive to Arenal. It felt good to relax on the padded seats.

"I'm hungry!" Junior announced. "As soon as we see a restaurant, let's stop to eat."

There were no objections. Hiking down all those steps had given us a pretty good appetite. Besides, the digital clock showed 1:00 p.m.

About ten minutes after we left La Paz Waterfall Gardens, we saw another beautiful waterfall in the distance. The falls dropped into tremendously deep ravine. We estimated that the drop from the road to the bottom of the ravine was approximately 4,000 feet.

Lewis pulled over and the rest of us got out of the

vehicle to view this magnificent sight. We spent a few minutes there, cameras flashing. Suddenly Lewis got an urge to get moving. He revved up the engine to get our attention. We jogged back to the vehicle.

As we got settled in, Lewis hurriedly shifted into gear and took off with an urgency, much faster than before.

"What's the rush? Let's slow down and enjoy Costa Rica," said Junior.

At 1:15 we passed some men working along the roadside. It looked as if they were working on the side of a cliff. A portable concrete mixer stood very close to the edge.

"Now just what would those fellows do if the earth would start shaking?" Leroy wondered. Our conclusion was that probably the safest option was to crawl inside the concrete mixer.

I chuckled to myself, imagining that old concrete mixer bouncing to the bottom of the ravine, with a man riding inside. Five minutes later my perspective would change drastically. This would be no chuckling matter.

We passed these men five minutes before the earthquake struck. Most likely these men were buried in the landslide and are in eternity now.

Chapter Three

Earthquake!

By now our empty stomachs really were rumbling. We were all on the lookout for a place to get a good helping of chicken, rice, and beans. Surely there would be a restaurant in Cinchona.

Indeed, there was a small restaurant named La Estrella. Yet, not one of us saw this place. Seven hungry boys, looking for a meal, drove right past it!

To keep our minds off our growling stomachs we decided to sing our theme song, "Let My Life Be a Light". We sang out the melody clear and sweet.

> *Let me live, blessed Lord in the light of thy word.*
> *Let my life be a light on a hill*
> *Leading souls now astray to the straight narrow way*
> *Help me do some good deed while I live.*

Chorus:
Let my life be a light shining out through the night.
May I help struggling ones to the fold.
Spreading cheer everywhere to the sad and the lone.
Let my life be a light to some soul.

Give me wisdom and power, every day every hour.
Let me drink from the fountain above.
Guide my footsteps aright, through the dark stormy night.
Give me peace, give me joy, give me love.

Give me souls for my hire, let my life be on fire
Shining out to the world as a guide.
Help me rescue someone, sinking now with no hope
That in heaven we shall ever abide.

The strains of our theme song faded, and each was lost in his own thoughts. Yes, our prayer was that opportunities would arise in which we could be a shining light for God. We were hungry, but for the moment, enjoyed each other's company. Before too long we would surely find a place to eat. Our trip was off to a great start.

We drove through the town of Cinchona and continued north toward Cariblanco. We passed a lane that lead up from the road to a large building. Apparently it was some factory. Next we rounded a hill where tall, multicolored red and green plants formed a hedge to our left. The SUV followed the ribbon of highway at a leisurely 35 mph.

The digital clock showed 1:21 p.m.

Without warning, our smooth traveling was interrupted by a terrifying lurch. A unseen force seemed to be pushing the SUV toward the middle of the road. It swerved two feet left of its intended course, tilting violently.

Cre-e-eak. Crash! Metal rattled as the house beside us shuddered, then collapsed. Plants from the hedge swayed and fell.

Jeremy looked left and right. Where is this mighty wind coming from?

"What!?" thought Leroy. "Is Lewis pulling off a stunt to scare us?" He glanced over and saw Lewis desperately gripping the steering wheel, his face stricken with panic. Leroy's mind whirled. Lewis was not playing a prank. Something was drastically wrong.

Lewis tried his best to keep control of the vehicle. He braked hard and the wheels stopped moving, but a mysterious, powerful force continued to rock our SUV.

Then, like a deep-sea wave rolling toward us, the road rippled up and down, up and down.

The house beside us collapsed with a crash!

Sections of the road rose twelve inches then partially settled down again.

"A front tire has blown," I thought, from my back seat viewpoint. But it didn't make sense! The vehicle was stopped and we were still rocking around.

Lewis was speechless, until he saw the earth moving. "Earthquake!" he shouted.

Instantly, Jeremy, too, realized that we were caught in an earthquake. "What, oh what should we do?" he thought.

For twenty seconds we sat helplessly while the vehicle rocked like an amusement park ride that was out of control. We teetered from side to side, then from corner to corner.

The SUV swung hard to one side, then to the other. Suddenly it was balanced on two wheels. Oh, no! Would we flip over? For one breathtaking second we hung in the balance of uncertainty, then relief! The Toyota settled back onto all four wheels.

Thump, thump. A dangling suitcase bumped against the window.

"Lord, help us! Keep us safe," Junior pleaded earnestly.

Jon Anthony joined in, "Lord, forgive us where we have failed."

My heart longed to pray, too, but no words came to my mouth. I was stunned. My dense mind was slow to grasp the seriousness of this earthquake. Soon I would wake up to reality.

Should we stay in the vehicle or should we get out? We were not sure where we were the safest. Electric lines dangled dangerously above the vehicle. The road seemed fairly intact ahead and behind us. Still, we decided it would be safest on the highest point of the hill. We backed up to the top of the hill.

Crush, crush, crush. The wheels flattened the fallen stalks from the hedge.

We sat silently, not knowing what to do next. We didn't know it then, but we had just been in the very epicenter of the earthquake that measured 6.2 on the Richter scale. The earthquake was fourteen kilometers deep.

Many questions raced through our mind. "Of all things, experiencing an earthquake on our trip to Costa Rica! What will happen next, Lord? What are you trying to teach us? Will something good come out of this experience? Lord, increase our faith."

Junior opened the door and placed one foot on the pavement. Just then the ground vibrated with aftershocks. His foot jerked forward, backwards, and left and right. Quick as a flash he brought it inside again.

A little later the ground seemed more stable again and we decided to get out of the vehicle. The luggage was still all on the top of the vehicle, except for one suitcase dangling down over the side. The SUV showed no signs of damage, even though the spring suspension had been tremendously tested.

We gathered in a circle, hands on the shoulders of the ones beside us, pleading earnestly for God's protection. Along came a tremor that nearly knocked us off our feet, but we were knitted together in a tight circle. (This secondary tremor measured 4.3 on the Richter scale.)

As we staggered to regain our balance, we were surprised to see dozens of people streaming toward us. According to their uniforms, they were from some factory. The men were wearing blue and the women were in pink. Most of them wore knee high white boots.

They walked rapidly past us, seeming to have a destination in mind. Many were dazed and clinging to each other. Some were crying. We heard a flurry of frantic Spanish.

We decided that we might as well follow the crowd. Maybe they could lead us to safety. We drove slowly down the road, keeping pace with the crowd of workers. Just in front of us was a small light blue van marked *Turismo*. A man was driving with a little girl sitting in the front passenger seat.

We came up to the place where some of the road was

broken off. There was a vehicle parked in the opposite lane right across from the broken off section of road. We needed to squeeze through a lane only eight feet wide.

Junior got out of vehicle to do the directing for Lewis. He stood on a mini landslide where ten feet of bare dirt was exposed. We were right between the other vehicle and the broken off section of road when a tremor started. Junior lost no time getting back to the solid road. Lewis quickly trumped on the throttle and hurried through to the other side. We made it through safely. What a relief!

By then we realized that it was not safe to keep driving. The man in the little blue van rolled down his window, and said "We better get off the road. It is not safe!"

Oh, good. Here was someone who spoke English. The man guided his vehicle into a private lane then beckoned us to park behind him. We were not too sure about parking our vehicle on another person's property. But we decided to trust his judgment. Some workers from the factory were walking around at the lane where we parked

"My name is Frank," the man told us. "My daughter and I just escaped from the El Angel factory!"

We learned that the workers in blue and pink uniforms worked at this large factory. There was major damage to the factory including a landslide that blocked the road to Cinchona.

We had followed Frank's advice to park our SUV, but we did not know what to do next. We longed to contact our families at home. Repeatedly Jeremy checked for signal on our cell phone. Repeatedly the display flashed that there was no reception.

We were quite shook up emotionally and physically. To experience an earthquake was totally unlike anything we had ever faced before. Will there be another hard earthquake? Where was the safest place to go? Should we keep following the factory workers? Amid our indecision there was one thing we could do. We could ask God to help us. He knew much more about earthquakes than we did. Our hearts cried to Him for wisdom.

It seemed like our best option was to walk to a safe place, maybe the nearby town of Cariblanco, and arrange for brethren from San Carlos to pick us up. We decided to worry about our rental vehicle later. The seven of us grabbed our bags and suitcases. Here we go!

Frank watched us preparing to walk with the crowd. "Please stay here," he pleaded. "The road becomes very steep down to the bridge. It is probably not safe!"

We considered his warning. Maybe it wasn't wise to start walking. Still, we dared to hope that somehow we could make contact with the brethren at San Carlos.

Chapter Four

Can We Walk to Safety?

When we left the vehicle, I was well aware of my energy shortage. For me, hiking is not an easy activity. My prayer was that God would give me strength for the path that lay ahead of me.

At first the walking was not too difficult because it was all downhill. But it was scary to slither under downed electric lines. In a few places we needed to take big steps across cracks in the pavement.

After walking down the road for about ¾ mile, we saw a small landslide ahead. Those at the front of the crowd scrambled up across the loose dirt and fallen trees until they could see beyond the blockage. Suddenly they let out a cry of dismay and start turning back and walking back up the road, the way we had come. By the looks on their faces, we were in a predicament. Someone informed us that just ahead the bridge on the Angel River was washed away.

I heard a lot of rapid and excited Spanish, which I wished so much I could understand. One thing we could understand that we were trapped. The bridge was out in front of us and major landslides near the factory blocked the road behind us. Trapped! What a dreaded word!

What could we do but to walk back up to where we had left the van? We groaned to think of the long uphill walk before us. Once again we had to crawl across the tree branches and electric lines that lay in tangled ruins over the road. Here and there we even saw people resting on the downed electric lines. So apparently the lines were not hot. We felt tremors every eight to ten minutes. It was important to be on the constant lookout for landslides and falling trees.

I was glad that Lewis was there to hoist my luggage over one of the fallen down trees. I was getting too weak to do much lifting. I walked up and down that road in the strength of the Lord. I had a level of energy that I did not know that existed. It seemed that I would wear down to a certain point and then God would give me strength for one step at a time. That is how God works. He gives us strength for one step at a time, and one day at a time.

Junior later admitted that he wept numerous times as we were walking back up the hill toward our vehicle. He knew we were trapped and there was no way out. What a deplorable situation. There was nothing to do but wait for help.

We gladly parked our luggage at the van again, and paused for a few minutes to catch our breaths. Then we noticed that many people were gathering up on a hill about three to four hundred yards from the road. On top of the hill, there was no danger of landslides. We would join the crowd.

Jeremy and Lewis were the first to venture up there. When they arrived at the hill, there was a group of about forty people gathered together in a circle praying. We were not the only ones who were beseeching the Lord. It was a blessing to see others pouring out their heart to God and asking Him to help them.

Junior said, "This is my opportunity to share something for Christ." He took his Bible along up to the hill.

We looked around and spotted Frank and his little girl. He gave us a wide smile and a thumbs up signal. He was very glad to see us! He feared for our safety after seeing us head down the road toward the river.

Quite soon we felt comfortable with Frank's judgment. I think he even trusted us more than we trusted him. He thought he might have a cell phone charger in his van that would fit our phone. He handed over his van keys, which were on a ring with many other keys.

Frank was a great help to us for translating. Only two or three others on the hill could speak English. It was a gift from God to have an interpreter who was on fire for the Lord. Frank had been a Pentecostal preacher at one time but now was a part of a non-denominational church. He was a tour guide and had been driving south to San Jose to meet some tourists. He and his daughter stopped to buy ice cream at El Angel factory when the quake occurred.

More and more people came walking up to the hill until a crowd of approximately 130 people were gathered there. Most of those gathered were factory workers and those who lived nearby. Some, like Frank, happened to be driving on this stretch of the road.

The rich owners welcomed us to come up on their property. The El Angel property consisted of two or three thousand acres. This included the El Angel factory, a dairy, a large house and a hydroelectric plant. The factory and hydroelectric plant were devastated. The house also suffered damage. One major crack went from the base of the house all the way up through the roof.

The owners experienced much loss and yet they seemed cheerful. A gray-haired woman who owned part of the property said, "We started from nothing, and I guess we can do it again." This definitely was a good attitude coming from the lips of an old woman. What would be my response to such a great loss?

There were over one hundred workers at the factory. Some of the workers were hurt, but none of them were killed. One boy was hurt very badly. A large roll of steel had fallen upon him, leaving him with a broken arm and leg, a hurting back, and an ugly wound on his forehead. He was carried up to the hill on a pallet. He moaned and groaned with much pain. He was given pain medication, but it didn't seem to help much.

The atmosphere among the crowd was tense. A number of the women were crying. Some did not know the whereabouts of family and friends. Some had seen landslides cover the houses of those they knew.

A group of us boys formed a circle to pray. We joined hands and took turns asking God to help us.

Andre noticed someone approaching. "Look, this man wants to join us," he told us.

A man with a striped shirt came up to our group and we included him in our circle. When it was his turn to pray, he began, "*Señor in el cielo...*"

We did not understand all he said, but we were

confident that he was praying to God. This experience was so precious to me. I understood very little, if any, of the words that he said, but I'm sure that God heard the prayers of each one. We could be united in the spirit of prayer without speaking the same language.

Frank Herrera Hendez

Andre, Lewis, Jeremy and Leroy in front of collapsed slabs of pavement.

Chapter Five

Hope of Rescue

It was not until two or three hours after the quake that we had cell phone reception. This was on the hill of El Angel. Jeremy called home and spoke with his father, Paul Weaver.

Paul listened with astonishment and concern as Jeremy told him the events of the past hours. He promised to start a prayer chain right away. It was a tremendous comfort to me to know that there are brothers and sisters praying for us.

We were very fortunate that we could get in contact with someone in the states. It was a relief to know that they could spread the word about our situation. Even though we had shocking news, no news from us would have been much more shocking. They could know that we were all alive and well. We were with a group of other stranded people, not alone somewhere in a remote area.

Not only were we concerned about getting word to our families, but also to Lewis and Jeremy's special friends. Lewis' fiancée, Malinda Lehman, lived in Michigan and Jeremy's girlfriend, Jennifer Miller, was from Martinsburg, Ohio.

Jeremy is calling home.

We locked the SUV and took the keys with us.

Soon after hearing about our plight, Paul Weaver sent an e-mail to family and friends:

Pray! Pray! The boys have experienced an earthquake in Costa Rica and now they are on the mountains stranded. The earthquake started while they were driving. They were on two wheels through part of the earthquake. Control was nearly lost of the vehicle due to the immense rocking of the ground. Nevertheless, the boys are not hurt, but they are shook up.

There is quite a bit of damage in the area. There are landslides and power lines down. Buildings have collapsed and some have slid down the landslide. There are tremors still shaking the earth.

They were hoping to walk out to safety. However, they discovered that the bridge is out and the river is too high to cross. They have no water to quench their thirst. No Spanish to communicate and it will be dark in a few hours.

Paul Weaver made contact with the Costa Rica brethren concerning rescue efforts. Paul also contacted his assistant, Kim Eichorn from Ohio, who had just arrived in Costa Rica on assignment for Christian Aid Ministries. Duane Nislys of Pital had been on hand to meet Kim.

Duane was able to call us and learned our whereabouts. He would do his best to see if there was some way for us to get to safety.

The earthquake changed everyone's plans. Duane and Kim along with Dale Heisey were planning to have a meeting. Instead of having a meeting, Duane and Kim were trying to rescue us. Junior told Duane it is too bad they could not have their meeting. But Duane informed him that they were so concerned about the stranded boys they would not have been comfortable proceeding with the meeting.

The following account was written by Duane and Ruth Nisly, of Costa Rica:

The week of January 4, 2009 began normal, but it did not end that way. On January 8, our family went to pick up Kim Eichorn from CAM, coming from Nicaragua. Everything went well and we met him coming through the border. Ruth was talking on the phone with Maureen who started shrieking, "The ground is shaking!" That is how we found out something was happening.

A little later we stopped at a restaurant for some lunch. On the news, they were showing some evidence of the 6.2 magnitude earthquake. They were somewhat nonchalant about it, so we thought it was not much to worry about.

After we spoke with our son Randall at the Imprenta we knew that earthquake indeed was a serious matter.

The whole country of Costa Rica felt the shaking. Ruth's dad said that the good shaking disturbed his afternoon nap.

When we arrived at Lake Arenal, we received a call from someone in the States. We were informed that the seven young men we were expecting for Sunday were trapped close to Cinchona. We found out that the road from Vara Blanca to Cariblanco was a complete disaster. At different places, there were landslides over the road, trapping people at various different places. Although we did not have many details, they were wondering if we could do something to help.

We tried to communicate with the young men, but their cell phone was almost out of power. We then decided to go up to Cariblanco and see how close we could get to them. We discovered that the bridge without sides on the corner was missing. Landslides kept on sliding into the river, temporarily causing a dam. The dam held up for a while. When the dam would break there would be a great avalanche of water, trees, and mud destroying anything or anyone in its path.

What really alarmed me was that there could be avalanches on the Sarapiqui River that could do a lot of damage to the people below in La Virgen and Puerto Viejo area.

As it looks from the aerial photos, that El Angel has received much damage. The little Soda El Campisino has received much damage. This indeed looked like a great disaster area. Yet God is always in control so we can rest in Him.

Paul Weaver contacted his assistant Kim Eichorn and asked him to see if they could organize a rescue. Kim told him that we would try. However, if it was not possible to rescue them now we would try again in the *morning.*

The warm afternoon sun beat upon us as we sat on the hill of El Angel and evaluated our situation. We were stuck. We needed to totally depend on someone else to help us. The roads were impassable. Our monetary means were not sufficient to rescue us. We felt quite helpless. Despite all this, we knew there was Someone watching and caring for us. He wanted to take our impossibilities and make them possible.

Many questions were unanswered at the time. What about food and water? Where will we sleep for the night? Lord, what are You trying to teach us? What can we do but trust in Your control?

As the day progressed it looked more and more like we would be stranded overnight. At approximately 4:15 p.m. a group of us boys gathered in a circle to pray.

"Dear God, have mercy on us. We ask for a means of rescue, if it is Your will."

We felt so forlorn. We did not see any sign of help coming as of yet. Frank had been instrumental in contacting emergency services, but only time could tell when and how quickly they would respond.

We took turns to pray and when the second person was praying we heard a sound in the distance. Our heads jerked up. Did we dare hope...?

Clup, clup, clup, clup. Yes, a helicopter! Our prayer was being answered! Louder and louder the craft came closer. It was the most beautiful sound we had heard all day. Many hands waved eagerly as the crowd watched the helicopter fly directly over us.

Here we were praying for deliverance, and just then a helicopter came along and flew over us. To me, this was a tremendous encouragement. Even though God is so big and powerful, He takes interest in our needs.

34.

This is just one of the many miracles that God performed. We thanked Him for showing Himself strong on our behalf. Truly God does as He promised in Isaiah, *And it shall come to pass, that before they call, I will answer; and while they are yet speaking, I will hear. Isaiah 65:24*

Now a different helicopter was nearing. We were overjoyed to see another beautiful bird flying in the sky. The helicopter pilot banked the copter and waved to the crowd. Hallelujah, they spotted us.

Air traffic was on the increase. Shortly before dark we heard another helicopter coming in low, but we couldn't see it. A hill blocked our view. The noise of the motors increased as it approached. Surely it would be here soon. Suddenly a blue and yellow helicopter hovered right above us and prepared to land!

Many hands waved eagerly as the first rescue helicopter appeared.

Chapter Six

Help Arrives

The deafening drone of the propellers pounded in our ears, but joy swelled up in our hearts as we scattered from the landing spot. The spinning blades whipped up dirt and the leaves from the ground and we turned our faces away to shield our eyes from the swirling debris. The copter was barely landed before the door swung open. A man jumped out and barked several questions into the crowd, and several other Red Cross workers joined him.

We were relieved to see that attention was first directed to the badly hurt boy. The Red Cross personnel attempted to move him from the pallet to a stretcher. Every bit of movement caused him to moan so badly that finally they just shoved the pallet onto the helicopter. Hopefully he would get good medical help soon.

Two other wounded people were also lifted out that evening. One was a middle aged lady with a tear stained face whom they half carried into the helicopter. The other was a young fellow who apparently had hurt his leg. Two men hoisted him up.

That evening, our spirits were uplifted to see a complete arched rainbow. Part of that rainbow was still visible in the sky when the helicopter came to pick up the wounded. We gazed up to see the lovely band of colors surrounding the helicopter like a priceless picture frame. How encouraging to be reminded of God's abiding promises!

E-mail update by Paul Weaver, Thursday evening:

I just spoke with Duane Nisly. Kim Eichorn and Duane are trying to reach the boys from Cariblanco tonight yet. Nevertheless, if that is impossible, they will try again tomorrow morning when the sun comes up. The boys are thanking God for His protection. They saw a beautiful rainbow, which reminded them of God's promise. "The angel of the Lord encampeth around about them that fear him, and delivereth them" (Psalm 34:7).

A little while ago, a helicopter came and picked up three earthquake victims. They flew them to a hospital in San Jose then plan to return and pick up the women and children as well. However, it will be morning before they pick up the women and children.

United States helicopters are being sent from Honduras to help evacuate the hundreds of stranded people. There is a good possibility that they will pick the boys up tonight or early tomorrow.

As we were talking, Duane said, "The ground is

really shaking again. However, it is a lot worse up in the mountain where the boys are."

At daybreak tomorrow some of the Costa Rican brethren will try to reach the boys in hopes of helping them and bringing them to safer and more secure ground. Duane said this is the worst earthquake they had in years.

The country of Costa Rica has a tremendous shortage of helicopters. They have no army of their own. In 1956, they sold their war equipment. They wanted to be known as a peacemaking country and not be involved in war. They had only two helicopters that could carry nine passengers each. Now there were hundreds of people to be evacuated!

On Friday evening the Costa Rican government asked all owners of private helicopters to come and help them with the evacuation process. Seven helicopters showed up in response to their request. Most of these other helicopters were smaller than the two blue and yellow Costa Rican helicopters.

Sometimes we were told that we could fly out that night. Other times we heard that we might have to stay two nights. We did not know what to expect. We did not know when we would get out of there. Knowing that God knew when we would be rescued had to be sufficient.

Duane Nisly writes:

It was getting dark. We decided that the best thing we could do was wait until morning, and then go see what we could do to help the boys. In the meantime, we were able to make contact with the young men. We advised them to prepare for the night. They told us that they are fine and that they can spend the night there.

We told them that we would look for them in the morning at daybreak.

We also communicated with Paul and he was a little more at ease. However, I think he was still quite concerned. Rightly so, because three of his boys were stranded on the mountains of Costa Rica.

We really wished that we could have helped them on Thursday. However, we had no way of reaching them. We encouraged them to prepare to stay for the night. When morning came, we would do our best to try to rescue the boys.

Chapter Seven

A Night of Camping

We came to realize that we had no choice but to spend the night out on the hill. Even though our bodies cringed at the thought, we knew this would become reality.

Some of the men were getting ready to start a fire. They took wood siding from a barn for firewood. They found an old rusty barrel and cut some holes in the bottom for ventilation. Using a machete, they whacked the boards in shorter lengths. This provided some heat and a comforting glow throughout the night.

Many people went to bed hungry that night. I was amazed that I didn't feel very hungry, even after not eating for twelve hours. We had some Payday candy bars along, which really hit the spot. But I decided that if I was not hungry, I would not eat my scanty supply of food.

There was some water available but we doubted whether it was safe to drink and avoided it. My throat still felt moist. To not feel very hungry or thirsty was indeed a blessing from the Lord.

Later that evening there was opportunity to share the Word of God. Frank preached for a while. Then he turned to Junior and asked him to have some words for the people. Junior was quite unprepared. He spoke for ten to fifteen minutes. Looking back, he does not remember a word of what he said. The Spirit of the Lord was faithful and showed him what to share. Frank interpreted for him.

A tall, young fellow in a blue outfit followed the Frank and the boys, but he kept lagging behind in the distance.

Andre nudged Frank, "Ask that young man if he needs help."

With a bit of questioning, Frank found out that this tall fellow's name was Ivan Sanchez. Yes, he was a worker at the El Angel factory. He had been a Christian at one time, but now he was backslidden. Yes, he would like to someone pray with him. He wanted to get right with God again.

Frank, Junior, and Andre then prayed with Ivan, and there he rededicated his life to God. What a time of great rejoicing! We thanked the Lord for doing His

Jon Anthony, Ivan Sanchez, Junior and Frank

work in this young man's heart. The prayer of our hearts, expressed in our theme song, was being answered.

> *Let my life be a light shining out through the night.*
> *May I help struggling ones to the fold.*
> *Spreading cheer everywhere to the sad and the lone.*
> *Let my life be a light to some soul.*

We were thankful for this opportunity to present the Gospel, out here in the countryside of Costa Rica. As I looked up, even the moon reminded me of the greatness of God. It shone in its beauty that night, faithfully reflecting the light from the sun. There is beautiful parallel between the moon and the sun and between the Christian and the Son of God. Reflecting the light of the Son of God is an obligation of the child of God. Everywhere we go we need to be faithful in reflecting the Son of God. We were only doing our reasonable service as we shared the Gospel with others.

Leroy, Lewis and I went down to our vehicle and Frank's to sleep. Junior, Jeremy, Andre, and Jon Anthony stayed up on the hill of El Angel. They wanted to be up there in case help would come that night, but I think they also feared that a landslide would come down on our vehicle.

Up on the hill, the people huddled together, trying to stay warm. Finding a comfortable spot to rest was quite a challenge. Lying on the pavement was the bed for some that night. Some spread plastic down on the pavement then lay down, using the curb for a pillow. When it started raining, the piece of plastic was used as cover. Andre attempted to find a comfortable spot to sit. So he sat on a five gallon bucket and tried to get some sleep. Finally, he gave it up. It simply wasn't comfortable!

While Junior was lying on the pavement, a tremor came. It felt like his head shook one way and his feet shook the other way. Twelve hours after the earthquake, Junior's knees still shook.

Frank's little girl sat out in the rain and never cried. In fact, we never saw her cry throughout the whole ordeal. There was a strong bond between the two of them. Father and daughter were always together. Frank said that a 6.2 magnitude earthquake is no problem for his daughter while she is with him. That is the way she has always been. If she is with her father, everything is fine. Isn't that the way it is with our Heavenly Father? If we abide in Him, all is well.

During the night the ground vibrated with tremors every ten to fifteen minutes. We needed to commit our fears to God again and again. Several times we heard the dull rumble of landslides. Why did the ground keep sliding off the hillsides? The earthquake had weakened the stability of the earth. As the tremors continued to shake the ground, the partly loose ground would break away.

Trees and dirt slid off the mountainside and fell down into the river. This caused the river to dam up temporarily. Eventually the pressure got so great that a big mass of water, mud, and trees rushed down the riverside. The river was rerouted as the great mass of muddy water rushed along, carrying the bridge downstream.

There was mud washed up at least 100 feet higher than the water level of the river. It destroyed anything that came into its path including houses, vehicles, and people. There was no respect of persons as the angry mass of water flooded throughout the valley.

Smaller mudslides would temporarily dam up the river. It was hard telling when the dam would break and send a gush of water, mud, and trees down the river again. Because of these dangers, no one attempted to cross the river until Friday morning.

We used a piece of plastic to cover us from the rain.

Chapter Eight

Rest in Restless Conditions

As nightfall approached, my mental condition was declining. In my heart I knew, it was time to spend some time alone with God in prayer. Dwelling on the uncertainties did not bring rest to my soul. I needed to focus on God, not the problems.

There was a battle raging in my heart. I did not know when we could get out. I did not know if we would get out that night or if we would have to stay another night. However, one thing I knew is that God wanted me to give Him all the unknown things that lay ahead of us.

What was God's answer to this situation? His solution was this: "My child, give me your whole life. Just trust me even though you do not know how or when you will get help. Do not worry about the future, but just place your full trust in me and I will deliver you. My child, give me everything. This is the way to peace and comfort."

The Lord seemed to be telling me, "If you do not commit everything to me now, you will look back with regret. When you see my divine purpose and how quickly I provide a way of escape for you, you will wonder why your faith was so small."

In my mind, I could respond two ways to this situation. I could choose to question God or I could commit the situation wholly to His Almighty power. Two choices were before me, with two completely opposite results.

I wanted to know when we would be rescued. However, that was not an option. Trusting without knowing facts indeed is not easy, but it is an essential part of the Christian life. Knowing that my God knew when we would fly to safety had to be sufficient. When I gave God the whole situation that night, He blessed me with peace and joy beyond compare.

That night I got about five hours sleep, which was very good considering our situation. In the morning someone asked me if I was able to sleep soundly through the tremors. I am sure I slept through quite a few tremors. God provided a peaceful rest.

E-mail update by Paul Weaver, late Thursday evening:

The boys are now camping, sleeping, and praying tonight in the wild mountains of Costa Rica. There are 130 people stranded on the hill of El Angel. They built a fire to try to stay warm. Their phone battery is almost dead. Jeremy calls me at appointed times so he can turn off his phone. This is their only source of communication and soon the battery will be dead.

Chapter Nine

Morning Comes

Friday morning, January 9, dawned gray and damp. Lewis and Leroy were eager to go and take pictures this morning. They walked up and down the road to the damage.

A light drizzle was falling when I walked up to the other boys. Most of the crowd sat around, trying to keep dry under umbrellas and makeshift rain gear. Some walked around aimlessly. Everyone seemed relieved that the long, weary night was past and morning had come. The sun peeked out from behind a cloud and we saw another rainbow.

Duane Nisly writes:
Kim and I arrived at Cariblanco at 5:00 a.m. Friday morning. Indeed, we were desperately looking for the

boys. We tried to do what we could, however, our resources felt quite limited. We went on down past the restaurant in Cariblanco and saw people gathered together under sheets and blankets.

They told us what had happened. They were there waiting to hear news from their family members who were trapped above. They did not know where they were or how they were doing. Neither did they know if their family members were among the living or the dead.

They also told us about the big scare that went through the Angel River in Cariblanco. The big avalanche of water, mud, and trees went down the river. We were amazed as we listened intently to their stories! The air was filled with the smell of pure mud, a most disagreeable odor.

When the day began to dawn, we walked down to where the bridge was. Coming around from the lower side of the river, we could hardly believe our eyes. It is difficult to explain in words how one feels when he sees devastation like this. There was no bridge in sight. It was gone! The place that had looked so familiar to us was unfamiliar.

The earthquake had so greatly changed the lay of the land. We can hardly believe the devastation that we saw. However, reality hits again, that indeed the bridge is missing. We thanked the Lord for protecting the boys. We are very thankful that they were not on the bridge at the time of the earthquake.

The neighbors were saying that they do not think the bridge was washed away. They claim that a big tree up stream was apparently holding back the limbs that were coming down the river. However, they were vastly mistaken. There is no way a big tree could have held back the limbs. The thing is if there were a big tree *there, it would have washed down in the avalanche.*

After we returned to the restaurant in Cariblanco, we saw that emergency vehicles began arriving. We hoped that the helicopters would soon begin to rescue the people. What a joy when the first helicopter flew over us! We could see it go until it landed at the big yellow house at El Angel, the very place where the boys were stranded.

However, the boys would have to wait a long time to be rescued. The wounded were still being brought to safety. Then next the women and children would be rescued. As we considered the fact that there were still bringing out wounded, we wondered when the boys would be rescued. How we hoped that they could be rescued, but we were afraid our fears would become reality, the reality of being stranded another night.

E-mail update by Paul Weaver, Friday forenoon:

I spoke with Jeremy this morning. They got very little sleep last night. It rained throughout the night, only adding to the misery. The helicopters were planning to come in this morning and evacuate all of them and take them across the river to Cariblanco. Duane and Kim plan to be there by now waiting for the escapees. Jeremy will call me once they are safe on the north side of the river.

The only way for them to get out is by helicopter. I just got off the phone with Duane Nisly who is waiting in San Miguel where helicopters are bringing the stranded ones. First the wounded will be evacuated and then next the stranded women and children will be flown out. Last of all the tough masculine men will be flown out.

The helicopters are still bringing victims on

stretchers. If they are still airlifting the wounded, it may go a long time before the boys are rescued.

Duane said, "Keep praying. They have no food and no good water. Now we lost all communication with them, because their cell phone battery is dead. You need to thank God that they are still alive."

There are families waiting and watching as the helicopters drop people off. They have family and do not know if they are alive or dead. They are hoping that the helicopters will bring their loved one.

"It is unbelievable how it looks," said Duane. The road gave away and dropped hundreds of feet into the ravines. Vehicles and people are still missing. There are trees, road, vehicles, people, and mud in an avalanche. There are still more avalanches happening. The earth is still shaking periodically. Not only are the helicopters rescuing people, but they also shuttle in many rescue workers as well.

By now helicopters constantly crisscrossed the sky, making trip after trip to lift out the stranded from various places. Here at the hill of El Angel the women and children were being flown out first. Frank and his little daughter were flown out together. Before we parted he gave his phone number to Junior. He wanted to keep in touch.

A group of ten Red Cross workers and some National Police came up on the hill. They were a very muddy sight due to their treacherous journey across the river. Here they organized a search for other stranded people, then headed into the countryside in smaller groups.

For breakfast we munched some delicious fruitcake that was gotten from the El Angel factory. It tasted so good because we did not have much food to eat in the last twenty-four hours. I decided I had better not eat too much food too quickly. Even though I felt like eating more, I didn't.

The fruitcake came in sealed packages, so we knew it would be safe to eat. But we were in a real predicament concerning the water supply. We had been told to avoid tap water and drink only bottled water. Now they were bringing five gallon pails lined with plastic bags up to the hill. We were informed that this water came from an old house nearby.

At first the water looked appetizing. However, there was a lack of cleanliness to dip the water out of the buckets. Cups were grabbed by muddy hands and dipped into the buckets to pour water into other cups. As one person after the other filled their cups, more and more floaties contaminated the whole bucketful.

Even if we could get water from the buckets before dirty specks were added, we were taking a risk because it was not bottled. Now, worse yet, people's hands are being washed while they were getting water out of the buckets. Surely we could endure thirst for a little longer rather than swallow that stuff!

Finally, we knew we needed to drink water. It was more than twenty-four hours since we had water to drink. We were possibly dehydrated more than we recognized. But the water conditions were not good. What a dilemma!

At last Junior declared, "I will either die from drinking water, or I will die by not drinking water!"

Most of us followed his lead and decided to risk drinking that water despite its questionable quality. We tried to avoid the particles as we dipped it out.

A report was circulating among the crowd that US helicopters would come in fifteen minutes. Fifteen minutes came and went and there was no sign of any US helicopters. After several hours we concluded that this report was inaccurate.

One man told us that we might be rescued late in the day on Friday. Another person said we may have to stay there another night. We didn't know what to believe. Finally I decided that there was no use in getting our hopes too high. When we were getting a ride in a helicopter, then we could know that we are being rescued. Until then we could only wait patiently.

On the other hand, we knew that something had to speed up dramatically or we would still be there for another night. This was not our favorite thought. We were ready to get out of our trap.

A group of rescue workers are organizing to search for other survivors.

Chapter Ten

Can We Cross the River?

A tall Red Cross man was organizing a group to cross the Angel River. Rescue workers on the other side would take people to Cariblanco or San Miguel. A lot of the men and some of the stronger women went to cross the river. We considered joining the group, too.

The tall Red Cross man informed us bluntly, "Either your life or your luggage." His crude statement made us cringe, but we had to admit it was realistic. Each one of us had at least sixty pounds of luggage. We knew it be nearly impossible to wade through waist deep mud while packing out our luggage. Most of the people who planned to cross the river held a sturdy walking stick in their hand.

For now, we decided to stay on the hill, but Lewis

and Leroy wanted to see what a river crossing was actually like. We still entertained the idea of getting out by this route. If nothing else, tagging after the group would break the monotony of waiting around on the hill.

When they left, the helicopter was stopping in occasionally. There were five different groups of people stranded along the mountainside. About every fifth time we saw the helicopter, it would land in our group. First thing in the morning they were still working on rescuing the hurt and the weak ones.

The sun rose higher and higher into the sky and we still waited for rescue.

Suddenly Junior pointed to the sky. "Look! Here comes a white helicopter we haven't seen before!"

We waved at him and he actually landed. This was a banana farmer helping those in need. He used this helicopter on his farm and now he was out rescuing stranded ones. He could haul four people at a time. That was not much but it was still four people. Soon the Costa Rican helicopter and the banana copter were both steadily hauling people out.

Many times now we had watched as a helicopter landed and others climbed aboard to ride to safety. The crowd on the hill was getting smaller with each pickup, but there were still quite a number of people waiting for a ride. When would it be our turn? Would it be soon?

The Banana Helicopter

E-mail update by Paul Weaver, Friday afternoon:
"Keep praying! It is now afternoon and within six hours it will be dark again!"

Duane Nisly writes:
The boys' cell phone battery was dead. We were only able to exchange a few words with them on our way up from San Miguel. We could not speak with them anymore. We did not know how or when they would be rescued. The Red Cross personnel told us that everyone who was stranded would be taken to San Miguel.

After waiting approximately three hours, we talked with the Red Cross officials. They told us that they were doing all they could, but they probably would not be able to rescue all the people that day. That was a great disappointment to us!

How we wished the boys could be rescued. As much as we tried to rescue them, our efforts were of no avail. It sounded like they may have to stay another night. We are hoping and praying they can be rescued today. However, we fear that the boys will have to spend another night on the hill of El Angel.

Now we did not know we should return to San Miguel or should we see if they would cross the river, I only wished there were some way that we could communicate with the boys. We had now lost connection with them due to their dead cell phone battery.

We then saw some people who had crossed the Angel River. You know, perhaps the people who have crossed the Angel River have seen the seven Americans. Upon closer observation, we noticed that those who cross a river are covered with mud. We inquired about the seven boys.

"Oh yes," was their reply. "We know exactly who you

are talking about."

"Well, do you know if they will cross the river or wait to be flown out by helicopter?"

Their reply was, "We do not know what they plan to do."

We were thankful indeed to hear that the boys are safe. However, the question still baffled our mind. "Where is the best place to meet the boys? Will they cross the river, or will they be flown out by helicopter?"

"Lord, show the way for us to go. We indeed need your guidance and help. We do not understand why you allowed the boys to experience this. We only ask that you would bring us together. We are so helpless. We depend on you, oh Lord, to bring the boys to safety."

We decided to go up to Angel River and wait for the boys there.

Down at the river, Lewis and Leroy saw that the helicopters were very busy.

"Say, the crowd up there must be thinning out fast," Lewis remarked.

"That's right," Leroy agreed. "It might be our turn to fly out soon. We better head up to the hill."

They turned away from the river and began their trek back to the hill of El Angel.

Duane writes:

When Kim and I got to the river, we saw a small crowd on the other side, but no sign of the American boys. We could hardly believe how the avalanche of mud had changed the scenery. This familiar place seemed like another world! It was incredible! Our mouths fell open, and we were almost speechless.

While waiting for the boys to cross the river, we saw that some people were crossing the river to go back to the stranded ones. We gave them a message to give to the boys.

For three hours we stood at the river bank, waiting for the boys to cross.

Finally I said, "You know, Kim, we been here for about three hours. Perhaps we should consider going to San Miguel again. We should at least get to higher ground where we have cell phone service. We should call home and see if they have any updates."

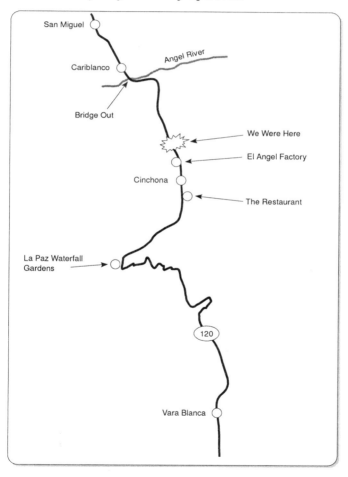

Chapter Eleven

Our Turn to Ride

The banana helicopter dropped off fresh pineapple, rice, and beans for the crowd on the hill. They also brought some good bottled water. As we sat eating, we looked around and realized that the crowd on hill was rapidly dwindling. Only some men and boys remained. It just might be our turn to go soon!

"Let's go down to the vehicle and gather up our luggage," Jeremy said.

"Where are the keys?" I wondered.

Jeremy drew in a sharp breath. "Oh, no. Lewis has them. And he's down at the river."

We scanned as far as we could see but there was no sign of the two boys. What if it was our turn to go and they still weren't back? Our hopes and prayers were that just any moment we would see them walking up to the hill. Again and again, we looked downhill. Where were they?

We walked around restlessly while the helicopters came and went several times. If only the boys would come back soon! If necessary, we would pass up our turn to go and wait until one of the last ones to fly out.

At last Leroy and Lewis came. Were we ever glad to see them!

The Red Cross personnel told us that because of our heavy luggage we could not all fly out together. This was fine with us. We'd gladly split up.

They told us that two or three could go along per trip with others who do not have luggage. Momentarily we decided which three would go out on the first trip and who would follow on the next two trips. I would go in the second group.

Soon the *clup, clup, clup* of a helicopter was heard in the distance again and our hopes rose. We were told that it was our turn to fly out. Oh, joy! As it came closer, we saw the familiar blue and yellow of the Costa

We are within 30 minutes of being flown out.

Rican copter. By now all of us had a greater appreciation for any helicopters.

"I'm hoping to get a ride with the banana chopper," Junior said. "I'll wait around until that one comes again."

The helicopter landed. The ones we had decided would go first - Jeremy, Jon Anthony, and Lewis - grabbed their luggage and headed toward the waiting aircraft.

Suddenly I noticed the man beside the door motioning me to come. Was there room for me on this trip after all?! I stepped toward the helicopter without delay. I could hardly believe that the thing I had longed for so long was now happening. Within minutes I would be free as a bird!

Andre sat on the grass, eating a juicy slice of pineapple, as he watched others board. He expected to wait for the last trip. Then he, too, noticed that the personnel by the helicopter were beckoning him to come. That good fresh pineapple suddenly held no value. He strode rapidly towards the open door. When Junior saw that all his comrades were on this helicopter, he gladly stepped aboard, too. Why wait for the banana helicopter?

Soon the motor was revving and the propellers whirled into action. The helicopter swayed gently back and forth as it lifted off the ground. With a roar it soared higher and higher in the sky. I looked around and, to my pleasure, all seven of us were in the helicopter. Tears of joy pushed at my eyes.

Junior burst out, "We have left behind the hill of captivity!"

Thank God! Finally our turn had come. We were rescued at last, after being stranded for 23 ½ hours and seeing so many others airlifted. I thought of the many other people who are stranded and still waiting for their ride out to safety. There are those who are hurting. Here I was in good condition and getting a ride to safety.

From our bird's eye view we could get a good perspective of earthquake damage in the immediate area. Now we clearly saw the large hole in the mountainside, formed by landslides. We could see this only part of this hole from the hill.

The gigantic hole in the mountain that was created by the earthquake.

"There's the El Angel River," Andre pointed out. We looked to see the wide swath of mud as it cut through the ravine.

The copter whirred above the mountains for a few minutes, then began its descent. The town of Cariblanco looked very inviting as we got closer and closer. The helicopter touched down in a grassy area near the road where some Red Cross workers were in charge. A mighty wind current from the propellers hit us as we stepped out. I hopped to the ground and got my luggage, then hurried away with my head bent low.

My heart sang: "Hallelujah, praise the Lord! I am free; I am actually free. Thank you, Lord for your goodness to me."

We are just dropped off and waiting to be taken to San Miguel.

Chapter Twelve

Meeting at Last

We waited at the curb with our piles of luggage. After a while a little four-door police truck pulled up. Would we like a ride to San Miguel? Yes, we did want a ride, but could we all get on this truck?

Three of the boys piled in the back seat. Four of us and all our luggage were crammed on the back of the truck. What a load! But we didn't care to be squashed for a little while. This was part of the rescue!

The overloaded truck motored five miles across the mountain range to San Miguel. Here we would meet the brethren at the city hospital.

We had heard that all the stranded ones would be given a medical examination at the hospital. We registered our names, but they did not even bother to check out our group. I think they saw that we were in fairly good shape.

Next we were directed over to some houses near the hospital where the Red Cross was serving cold watermelon and beverages. They had some of the best fruit flavored drink I ever tasted. I drank four glasses full. The other boys also gulped down glass after glass. It was so good to have a good, cold drink. They didn't seem to care about the amount of liquid we consumed. I'm sure they understood our cravings.

We were able to charge our cell phone at one of the houses. First thing we made a quick call to Ruth Nisly, letting her know that we had been flown out and were waiting at the hospital. She promised to let Duane know right away.

While we waited for Duane and Kim to show up, we watched as more and more victims were brought by ambulance and helicopter. Some were carried on stretchers. Others were unharmed. We watched with sadness as several body bags were unloaded.

A tense atmosphere prevailed as crowds milled around the hospital. Many were still hoping to see their friends and family among those who were brought in.

"Even with all the activity around here, I am amazed at how efficiently things are being handled," Junior remarked.

Duane Nisly writes:
After waiting about three hours, Kim and I decided to return to San Miguel. All the while, down by the river, we had no cell phone signal. I did not know that in the past hour my wife had been frantically trying to get a hold of me.

At home, Ruth sighed again after yet another

Andre, Jeremy and Jon Anthony Weaver

Samuel Beachy

Junior Troyer, Leroy Yutzy and Lewis Stutzman

*One of the many trails at
La Paz Waterfall Gardens*

At La Paz

Waterfall Gardens

La Paz Waterfall Gardens is a Birder's Paradise!

Andre is looking at the falls below with his binoculars. This was just briefly before the earthquake struck.

Before   *After*

We had visited these souvenir shops. Most of them were destroyed in the earthquake.

Here I am pictured standing by the lookout point pictured below. This was taken just briefly before the earthquake struck.

The lookout point below is totally destroyed.

Rescuers walk past two dead bodies.

*This is the house
that crashed right
beside us when the
earthquake started.*

*We were in front of
this house with a
green roof when we
finally got the
vehicle stopped.*

*The arrow shows our location when the earthquake started.
The house with a green roof is the building on the left. The
house that collapsed is where the arrow is.*

Here we are gathering up our luggage as the factory workers stream toward us.

We have to lift our heavy luggage over trees that have fallen over the road.

The roads were very treacherous with huge cracks and power lines strewn about.

*This is our moment of dreadful realization that we are trapped! The
people have just discovered the bridge is gone.*

*Jeremy is struggling to carry his luggage through a maze of trees and
power lines. A very discouraging time.*

Samuel, Jon Anthony, Junior, Frank and daughter, and Leroy. We are gathered on the El Angel hill waiting to be rescued.

This is the fruit cake and water that we had to eat and drink. The fruit cake was delicious, but the water was dirty!

Help is coming at last! The crowd is eagerly waving to the helicopter.

The helicopter has landed and will take the injured people first.

This man was seriously injured when he was hit by a coil of steel. He was suffering terrible pain.

Here they are preparing to load the injured man onto the helicopter.

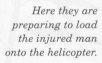

Here is a group attempting to cross the dangerous El Angel River.

The El Angel factory (above and left) suffered extensive destruction. At left is an aerial view of the factory.

The smashed and buried remains of the restaurant we passed.

Two men were killed and one man survived when they ran from their truck on the left.

An aerial view of the restaurant remains. Note the landslide covering the road. We had just passed by here minutes before.

Rescue workers dig for bodies at the restaurant.

Rescuers carry an injured woman to a safe zone.

A man weeps over the body of his cousin.

Red Cross personnel and Police officers transport a dead body.

Rescue teams search for bodies under a crushed house.

Many vehicles were smashed beyond recognition like this one.

Below is a photo of smashed houses created by the earthquake.

Above: Photos of landslides
Below: Photo of Duane and Ruth Nisly with some of us boys.

unsuccessful attempt to call Duane. How many times had she tried to call her husband? Knowing that seven boys were stranded had caused her enough trauma. Now she could not reach Duane to tell him the good news that the boys were at San Miguel waiting to be picked up. Where, oh where, were Duane and Kim? Were they lost or hurt? How she wished to be able to talk together!

Kim and I had just arrived at San Miguel where there was signal and we called home. When Ruth answered, her feelings of anxiety were nearly reaching their climax. All the pent-up emotions tumbled out as she cried, nearly shouted: "They are out and waiting on you!"

The intensity of her cry came partly out of relief to hear my voice. Apparently, there had been some tense hours while we had no communication.

What a relief to meet the young men, but the relief for them was much greater.

It is hard to express our great joy when we saw Phil Yoder, Ruth Nisly's brother, walking toward us. Within minutes Duane and Kim joined us. Oh, it was such wonderful meeting! Some of us had never seen these brethren before. However, instantly there was a common bond between us. Even though we had been with many others on the hill and at the hospital, it was a comfort to be with brethren of like precious faith.

We had just come through such a tremendously traumatic experience. At times it had been hard or impossible to make contact with these brethren. But now we were rescued and met each other face to face. It was an unspeakable relief.

Another Search Expedition

Not only were Duane and Kim trying to rescue us, but a few others were, too. Marvin, Ruben and Brian Dueck and Michael Schrock, made an expedition on Friday. Here is their story:

"Did you hear there are some boys stranded near Cinchona?"

"Oh really! Do you think we should go and look for them?"

"I have been wondering the same thing. Maybe we could possibly locate them."

"Yes, it would be great, if we could somehow find them."

We crossed the river near Cariblanco, and traveled by foot to Cinchona. We told the Red Cross personnel and the authorities that we would like to help uncover people. We were told that it is too dangerous to look for bodies now. The reason it was dangerous was the continual tremors. Also, all the rain had loosened the ground. The water would run down into the cracks and weaken the already unstable hillside. Landslides were still happening. Therefore, the rescue workers were cautious where they would dig up bodies. They did not want a landslide to bury them alive.

It gave us a scary feeling to stand right at the edge of a steep, deep ravine. We were a bit more cautious about where we went. The whole place, roads and everywhere was full of cracks, where the land did not slide off completely. The earth was quite soaked with all the rain we had been having.

When we were finally ready to go back, the rescue workers told us that it is too dangerous to go back across the river. That means we were stranded and needed to be airlifted. We got a ride back to San Miguel in a helicopter.

You know, it seems rather foolish that we went back to look for the boys and never found them. Then in the process, we became stranded and had to be flown out the helicopter. The boys whom we went to rescue were rescued before we were!

Chapter Thirteen

Weekend in Pital

With gratitude we arrived at Duane and Ruth Nisly's home Friday evening. Soon I thought of my family many miles away. So much had transpired since I had seen them last. I inquired of the costs to call home. The calling rate was a reasonable enough. After all, the cost of calling home did not matter that much to me.

I dialed the proper sequences to reach home. The phone rang a few times from the other end of the line, then someone answered. It was Mom!

"Mom," I said. "This is Samuel. It's good to hear your voice!"

"Samuel, it's so good to hear *your* voice." Mom's reply quavered with emotion. Both of us knew very well that it was only because of God's mercy and protection that we were speaking with each other.

What should we do about the SUV? Junior contacted the Alamo car rental agency in San Jose. They were overjoyed to hear that we were safe since they knew our planned route took us right through the quake stricken area. Their instructions were to leave the vehicle where it was parked. We were not to worry about it. Alamo asked us to bring the keys in to their office and they would give us another rental vehicle.

On Saturday, Duane and Junior made a trip to San Jose to get another rental vehicle. Later the boys went on a hike, but I stayed at Duanes' and wrote about our ordeal while it was still fresh in my mind.

In the evening Duanes and we boys went out to eat at a local restaurant. We saw news reports that focused on the earthquake damage. Scene after scene of damaged roads and houses flashed before us. The road between Cinchona and Vara Blanca was a complete disaster. The La Estrella restaurant that we had just passed was destroyed and fourteen people lost their lives.

Names of at least fifty missing people were listed. Most of these had likely perished in landslides. There were some people missing in the La Paz area, including two people from England.

Oh, no! Our thoughts went immediately to the friendly couple we had met at La Paz Waterfall Gardens. There were seven sober boys who realized how nearly our names could have been on that missing list.

Sunday morning we accompanied Duanes to Iglesia Menonita de Pital for services. First Duane preached a short sermon, then asked each of us to speak briefly. We didn't give much details about the earthquake itself or the damage that we encountered (most of the congregation knew those things already) but shared the feelings of our hearts.

In the evening a crowd of nearly three hundred people came together at La Estrella church to see our slides. All the Beachy Amish churches in Costa Rica were represented. Marvin, Brian and Ruben Dueck and Michael Schrock, who had set out from Cinchona to look for us, showed their pictures as well. They had pictures of one major landslide less than a mile behind us. Reality sank into our minds as we considered the great danger that was behind us. How closely death lurked behind us! How fortunate we were to still be alive! To a degree, we relived the earthquake experience.

After the slides, the seven of us sang our theme song. Our voices rang with feeling as we sang:

Give me wisdom and power, every day every hour.
Let me drink from the fountain above.
Guide my footsteps aright, through the dark stormy night.
Give me peace, give me joy, give me love.

God had heard this prayer. He had heard the prayers of the brethren and sisters assembled here. He had guided our footsteps aright with His divine timing.

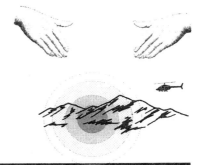

Chapter Fourteen

The Emotional Aftermath of the Earthquake

Monday morning came and we prepared to continue with our travels. But some of us were still trying to cope with an unsettling emotional aftermath. Fears and apprehension disturbed our sense of peace.

Immediately after the quake, our minds were mostly occupied with the thought of rescue. It was not until a few days later that the full reality of our near tragedy hit us. What if we had been caught in the landslide? What if we had not stopped to take pictures of the falls? What if we would have been driving on the bridge as it was swept away? The chain of events and possible events replayed in our minds again and again. We talked about the importance of committing everything to God and trusting Him for our every need.

Duane and Ruth accompanied us to Arenal on Monday. There we bid them farewell and resumed traveling on our own. First we spent two days sightseeing in the Arenal area. We enjoyed our time at the Caño Negro Wildlife Reserve and taking a river tour, even though the weather was mostly cloudy. One evening the clouds lifted and we got a good view of red hot lava spilling from Volcán Arenal.

I enjoyed being there at Arenal, but it was not without mixed feelings. It gave me a terribly uneasy feeling to stay at the base of an active volcano for two nights. I had already experienced an earthquake on this trip. Being there did not help the turmoil that was in my heart already. I would commit my life to God, but still I could not find rest and release.

On Tuesday night we heard more frightening news. There was some unrest in Nicaragua near Managua. Rebels had stopped a hundred vehicles north of Managua and started a fire on the road. This was on the very road we needed to travel to get from Managua to Waslala.

We were advised to wait a little to go to Nicaragua. Our lives had already been endangered one time and we did not feel like knowingly stepping into another dangerous situation. Our plans seemed to be falling apart again.

This trip was turning out so vastly different from what we planned. We did not know what plans to make. It seemed best to take one day at a time and follow the Lord's plans.

At this point, I was so ready to go home. It looked so appealing to forget the idea of going to Nicaragua. Some of the other boys were over their aftermath experience, but some of us were still struggled to find rest.

We decided to see what it would cost to change our

tickets to fly home from San Jose. The fee to have our tickets changed was four to five hundred dollars. Outrageous! That was simply too much to pay for changing our tickets! We took the expense of changing tickets as a confirmation that God wanted us to keep our plans of going to Nicaragua.

On Wednesday, January 14, we left Arenal, much to my relief, and traveled south toward the Pacific coast. We arrived at Puntarenas at 1:00 p.m.

Some of us boys strolled out to the beach. We kicked around in the sand and watched the waves rolling to shore.

Suddenly Junior sank onto the beach with an exhausted sigh. "I'm just plain worn out emotionally. Right now nothing seems more inviting than to go home."

That really got me worried. If Junior decided to go home, we would all need to go home. He knew more Spanish than any of us did.

By the next day God did work in his heart. Junior had found peace and courage and was ready to go to Nicaragua. I overheard him talking on the phone, telling others what great blessing it was to find release.

After his call was done, Junior turned to me. "Samuel, I have been delivered from the emotional aftermath, but have you?"

It cut me to the heart to recognize that he was at peace and I was not. I so badly wanted to find release. I had prayed to God to help me, but still I was not totally at peace.

"Lord, what can I do?" I cried. The Lord revealed what I needed to do. When Thursday night came, I went out on the back porch of the motel and spent an hour alone with God in prayer. I entrusted everything to God, my life, my future, and even my fears of going to

Nicaragua. I am reminded of Fanny Crosby's words from the third stanza of "I Am Thine, O Lord."

O the pure delight of a single hour
That before Thy throne I spend,
When I kneel in prayer, and with Thee, my God,
I commune as friend with friend.

The next day Junior asked me if I want to go back to Waslala, Nicaragua or if I just wanted to stay in Managua.

"I am ready to go to Waslala," I answered with confidence. "Listen to what happened last night." I told him about my hour of prayer, out on the back porch. God had heard my prayers and granted me peace and release.

"Bless the Lord," he said repeatedly as I recounted my experience.

Chapter Fifteen

To Nicaragua

After we left Puntarenas, we traveled north to Peñas Blancas on the border. Lucas and Julianna Miller and family from Managua were there to meet us. Since rental vehicles are not permitted to cross the border, the Millers took us across. We rented a vehicle in Nicaragua and followed Lucases all the way to Managua. Here Alvino Miller's son Samuel met us and went with us to Waslala. It was good to have someone with us who was familiar with the roads and the culture.

Was I ever glad we went to Waslala! It was such a good experience for us. We had a very enjoyable time of fellowship with Pablo Yoders, Tim Schrocks, and the Alvino Miller family. This uplifting weekend was the perfect ending for our trip.

On Sunday we attended morning services at Jicaral. In the evening we showed slides from our earthquake experiences at the church in Waslala. Once more, the seven of us sang fervently:

Let me live, blessed Lord in the light of thy word.
Let my life be a light on a hill
Leading souls now astray to the straight narrow way
Help me do some good deed while I live.

Chorus:
Let my life be a light shining out through the night.
May I help struggling ones to the fold.
Spreading cheer everywhere to the sad and the lone.
Let my life be a light to some soul.

Give me wisdom and power, every day every hour.
Let me drink from the fountain above.
Guide my footsteps aright, through the dark stormy night.
Give me peace, give me joy, give me love.

Give me souls for my hire, let my life be on fire
Shining out to the world as a guide.
Help me rescue someone, sinking now with no hope
That in heaven we shall ever abide.

When we had left home ten days earlier, all of us wanted to let our lives shine for God as we traveled. Little did we dream of all the ways in which God would arrange the timing, the places, and the people amid highly unusual circumstances. His ways are beyond our comprehension.

On Monday we traveled back to Managua with

Samuel as our guide once more. The six Ohio boys had a flight to Miami and then to Ohio. My flights were first to San Jose, then to Miami, then to Tennessee.

We could hardly believe that our travels together were nearly over. We were going home! Home to our waiting family and friends! Oh, wouldn't we have a lot of things to tell about our trip!

Chapter Sixteen

Facts About the Earthquake

These facts were released from news sources the day after the earthquake:

The US Geological Survey rated the earthquake as having 6.1 magnitude on the Richter scale, revising the initial figure of 6.2. Witnesses say that they had not felt such a strong earthquake in 30 years. The quake was so strong that it shook water out of the swimming pools.

The epicenter was twenty miles north of San Jose, but the quake was felt across the entire country of Costa Rica. It damaged 42 communities as well as their electric networks. The quake was followed by 800 tremors. Neighboring Nicaragua felt the quake as well.

"Today is a day of mourning for the Costa Ricans, because three people have lost their lives," President

Oscar Arias said Thursday afternoon shortly after the quake. An early report said that two children and a woman were killed and scores were injured.

A spokesperson for Red Cross said, "Access to Vara Blanca and Cinchona has been destroyed, due the serious road damage. Officials warn of potential landslides in mountainous areas, especially near the epicenter where tremors continue to shake the earth. Serious damage to infrastructure, roads, and homes has been reported."

Residents telephoned the local radio programs to report injured people in need of urgent medical attention. Some people were injured and trapped in their own houses. Many rescue workers endangered their own lives to save others.

The emergency commission declared a red alert in the capital and surrounding areas. San Jose's International Airport briefly suspended all flights. Public buildings, including the finance ministry, were evacuated. Many people ran into the streets immediately after the quake. San Jose residents reported broken windows and cracks in buildings. Roads were also damaged.

Costa Rica registered more than 4,700 earthquakes/tremors in 2008. Most of these were small tremors. According to the observatory, sixty of these quakes were felt by the population. A minor quake shook Costa Rica on Wednesday, just one day before the big earthquake. It caused no injuries or property damage.

By late Thursday evening the death toll rose to 15 with 100 missing, and 208 injured. Most of those 100 missing people were presumed dead. The landslides were so massive that it was impossible to find all the bodies. Some people have family members that simply disappeared. It must have been a very great day of mourning for the Costa Ricans.

Chapter Seventeen

God's Divine Protection to Us Seven Boys

On that Thursday morning, we had no idea how closely death lurked behind us. All the places we visited were at high risk for earthquake damage. La Paz Water Gardens, where we spent two and a half hours, was very much in the danger zone. We came from Poás, which was also a danger zone. At the time of the earthquake we were driving through a danger zone as well. Yet God graciously protected us.

Even though we were in such dangerous territory, God performed a miracle by keeping us safe. It is of the Lord's mercies that we are still living. We found ourselves right in the center of God's will in the epicenter of the earthquake.

We serve a great big wonderful God. He revealed

more of His all knowing power to us. Even though He is big, He takes interest in our lives. At the time of the earthquake, He took notice of that white Toyota SUV which had just passed the town of Cinchona. He allowed us to be at a safe place at the time of the quake. He noticed that SUV being tossed about on the road and was about to turn over on the side. He noticed the major landslide less than a mile behind us. He chose not to start the quake two minutes earlier.

If God had wanted to take us home, He would not have had to do anything out of the ordinary. He could have allowed us see the restaurant. He could have allowed us to be driving a mile farther back. If we would have stayed longer at La Paz Waterfall Gardens, or had stopped at the La Estrella restaurant, or if we had not spent a few minutes taking pictures of the falls, the outcome of our earthquake experience would have been so drastically different. Possibly our bodies would have been flown back to the United States in wooden boxes. Worse yet, we could have been buried in a landslide. It is terrible to envision all the sad possibilities, but I recognize that this could have been reality. For many others, it was reality.

Yes, God vividly demonstrated His protection to us. The timing was divine. The location was divine. Repeatedly I recognize that it was God's will for us to remain safe. God could so easily have allowed to be in a different place at time of the quake. But God is in always in control. God gives us life and breath, but he also controls the day of our death. I must conclude that it was not our time to die.

Why were we protected? Was it because we had some earned some special favor with God? No, absolutely not. There was nothing we did to deserve protection. It was simply the goodness of God.

I thank the Lord for allowing us to have this soul-searching experience. God wanted us to see His hand in all this. Knowing that my life could have ended, yet was saved, behooves me to serve God more faithfully each day.

Duane Nisly writes:

The boys decided to spend a weekend with us, relaxing and dealing with their fraying nerves. We spend a lot of time reflecting on the goodness of God, praising and glorifying Him.

It was also an important time reflecting on the purpose God must have for each of the young men, since He so miraculously saved them. It was a weekend of much reflecting for everyone.

One thought that forcefully dawned on me was that God could have opted not to save their lives. That would not have in the least degree altered His power and sovereignty. Just as God prompted them to leave the waterfalls in a hurry, and thus saved them from being buried by a landslide, God could have had them be detained long enough that the embankment would have carried them to a burial in the ravine.

The ways of God are much higher than our ways and His sovereignty never changes. Praise God for saving them! Could we have praised God if He would have taken them?

Let us look at some specific ways that God protected us that Thursday.

Volcán Poás National Park
We fully intended to spend time in Volcán Poás National Park, but changed our mind due to the cloudy weather. At first we were disappointed about having to

miss out on seeing the crater. Later we realized that the clouds were part of God's leading to get us out of a danger zone. The quake triggered many landslides in rural areas near Poás. It also tore apart a highway near the park. A number of people were killed and missing. Still we are safe and unhurt, even though we had just traveled on the highways near the park.

La Paz Waterfall Gardens

When we first came to La Paz Waterfall Gardens, we thought the price for a ticket was too high. Then we went down to the road to the bottom of the hill where we could view some of the waterfalls. This glimpse convinced us that we should reconsider and go back to the park entrance. I was at peace with this decision.

From 10:30 a.m. to 1:00 p.m. we walked the trails and explored the tropical beauty. There was no sign of impending danger, except for the peculiar behavior of one monkey. It was gnawing frantically at wire netting of the cage. We noticed this, but didn't guess that perhaps it sensed the coming quake. Perhaps an instinct was telling it to get out of there.

Less than half an hour after we left La Paz Waterfall Gardens, we were experiencing a 6.2 rating earthquake. How did the earthquake affect the Gardens? What happened to the tourists that were there? We hoped to find out.

At San Miguel we met a worker from La Paz Waterfall Gardens. He said that the workers all survived the earthquake, but some tourists were missing. On Saturday evening, two days after the earthquake, we saw on a news report that two people from England were among the missing.

The Gardens suffered much damage. Most of the parking lot slid down the hill, burying anything in its path. Landslides destroyed the animal houses and trails. The souvenir shop I had just purchased postcards was destroyed. The falls no longer had their unique beauty. Instead of the rushing clear water, the falls now were a muddy brown. The restaurant and the park reception building were the only building that were not destroyed.

The bridge where we had stopped to see the lower falls was still intact, but most of the little shops across the road were demolished by landslides.

I shudder to think we were walking in a death trap for two and half hours that forenoon. We could have easily been at the Gardens at the time of the earthquake.

After we were stranded, I had wished that we had not gone back to La Paz Waterfall Gardens. We could have driven far enough to the north to avoid this whole mess. We could have avoided the terror of shaking ground beneath us. We could have avoided being stranded on a hill for a part of two days, yet I believe God wanted us to encounter these situations. He had a mission in mind when we turned around and went back to visit the Gardens. If it was not God's will for us to experience the earthquake, why did I feel at peace about our decision?

The Waterfalls Near Cinchona

About ten minutes we left the La Paz Waterfall Gardens, we saw another scenic waterfall in the distance. A clean white spray plunged into a deep ravine, with lush green trees all around. We pulled to the side of the road for a few minutes. Some of us got out and took some pictures. Suddenly Lewis had an urge keep going and trumped on the throttle to get the attention of Junior, the photographer. We hopped into the vehicle and took off at a faster pace than before.

Unknown to us, these falls would change drastically only 15 minutes later. The thing of beauty became a scene of damage. Due to massive landslides around the falls, it was no longer surrounded by green trees. The lovely white spray was replaced with a muddy, brown flow. Quite likely we were the last ones who captured the original beauty of these falls with cameras.

Had we lingered there a few minutes longer, we could have been caught in a major landslide. What if we would not have stopped at the falls? Possibly we would have been driving across the bridge on the Angel River at the moment of the quake. That was definitely no place for safety!

The Restaurant

Soon after we left the La Paz Waterfall Gardens, Junior suggested that we look for a place to eat. I remember thinking that a platter of rice and chicken would be a delicious meal. Soon after that, the thought of eating slipped my mind.

We passed La Estrella restaurant in Cinchona less then a mile before the earthquake started. None of us saw the restaurant, even though there were seven people in our vehicle looking left and right for a place to eat.

Why did we not see the restaurant? Was it because we were sidetracked and not paying attention? No, we believe it was part of God's divine plan to save our lives. God had shielded our eyes to the sight of the restaurant. We had full intentions of stopping somewhere soon to enjoy some delicious food.

Just what happened to La Estrella restaurant? It was completely destroyed! It was buried in a landslide! Fourteen people were killed.

After the earthquake I began to meditate, "We didn't even have lunch yet. I wish we had stopped somewhere to eat. I sure could use a plateful of food to boost my energy levels." Little did I think, that had we stopped to eat at the restaurant, we would have perished before we could have satisfied our hunger. My thoughts of wishing we would have stopped to buy lunch now seem so foolish. I realize that I am privileged to be alive.

Our Location When the Quake Began

As we consider what happened ahead of us and behind us, we could not have been at a better place at the time of the earthquake. The mile and a half stretch of road that we were on was the ideal place. We were driving on top of a ridge. There were no major landslides within a few hundred yards of us.

At the start of the earthquake, a strong force moved our vehicle two feet to the left. Fortunately, we were pushed toward the center of the road. We are very thankful that this force did not move the vehicle the over the edge of a steep drop off.

Now imagine with me for a moment how things could have very easily happened to us.

Suppose our vehicle veers toward the ditch. It slides over the edge of the drop off, and is overturned. It tumbles end over end, down, down, down to the gully below. Glass shatters and metal bends. The vehicle loses its looks of identification. There is screaming. There is no hope of escape. Death is near.

Chapter Eighteen

God's Divine Protection to Others

Other people also had narrow escapes. We saw number of vehicles setting on the road with little damage. God's divine protection was very evident in their lives.

Richard and His Jeep

On the hill of El Angel, we met a man named Richard who had been driving his Cherokee Jeep down the road near Cinchona at the time of the quake. The ground shook, and *whoosh!* The road slid away beneath him. He was riding one of those dreadful landslides! Down, down, down. But then, the dirt stopped sliding. Richard surveyed his location halfway down the mountainside. Quickly he jumped out of his vehicle and scrambled over the loose, unstable soil back up to the road.

When he reached the safety of solid blacktop, he turned to look down at his Jeep. What do you suppose he saw? The ground was sliding again! The Jeep that he had just left minutes ago was rolling down the steep terrain into the gully. The vehicle was being devastated before his eyes.

Richard and Andre

Thankfully, he was not in the vehicle, heading for the end. The Lord had given him an opportunity to escape. He had been just seconds away from death's door. Richard stated, "If it was not for God, I would not be alive!"

Frank Herrera Hendez

Our friend Frank and his daughter were going to San Jose to pick some people up at the airport as part of his tour guide job. He asked his daughter if she wanted to stop for ice cream at the El Angel factory. She said that she really does not want ice cream.

Later, when they were nearer to El Angel, Frank's daughter said, "Papá, I would like to have ice cream after all." While they were at the factory, the earthquake occurred. Frank tried to stay close to his daughter as they rushed toward an exit. The ground was heaving and shaking and debris was flying all around them. Due to the chaos, he and his daughter were separated through part of the earthquake, but both of them arrived at their vehicle safe and unhurt. They were among the first escapees of the El Angel factory.

Where would Frank have been they would not have stopped for ice cream? We do not know whether he would have lived to tell his story. He would not have been on the hill of El Angel, helping others. Frank was a great blessing to us. He was one of the few people who could speak both English and Spanish. His involvement in calling the emergency services was greatly appreciated. We thank the Lord for bringing Frank and his seven year old daughter to the hill of El Angel.

The Bus

One man was driving a large bus at the La Paz Waterfall Garden area at the time of the quake. He was swept off the road and rode his bus down the landslide.

The bus flipped onto its side.

In spite of the grave danger he was in, he survived without receiving much physical harm. In fact, he only received a scratch on his shin!

The bus that rolled down the landslide.

Costa Rican Tourists

Since Costa Rica is a popular tourist destination, hundreds of people from other countries were affected by the quake. Hundreds of tourists experienced something that they will probably never forget. Approximately 300 tourists were trapped in a luxury hotel near Poás. More than 200 tourists were visiting a resort at La Paz when the road was destroyed, leaving them stranded. There were forced to seek shelter outside that night.

A group of six British volcanology students with three Costa Rica guides were inside the crater of the Poás volcano when the earthquake struck. They were all unharmed.

Three Men and a Box Truck

At Cinchona there were three men riding in a box truck near the La Estrella restaurant. When the earth started shaking the driver quickly stopped the truck. He jumped out and ran behind the truck. He was one of the fortunate survivors.

The two passengers got out and ran ahead of the truck. They were also hoping to run to safety. However, they ran right into the path of a landslide, which buried them alive. The box of the truck received some damage, but the cab still looked in good condition. For them it would have been better to stay in the truck.

God could have inspired the two passengers to run behind the truck to safety. It does not always matter so much the dangerous situation we are in. Sometimes it mostly depends on whether it is the person's time to go or stay. God's timing is the best timing for us regardless of the outcome.

Chapter Nineteen

God's Divine Will Meant Death to Some

We thank the Lord for His divine protection to us. We could easily have been among those for whom God's divine will meant death. Let us now look at what happened to some of the people that died.

The Couple from England

We heard from news reports that two people from England were missing in the La Paz area. Our hearts were saddened to realize that this was undoubtedly the friendly couple we had met at the Waterfall Gardens. Less than an hour before the quake we had been walking the trails with them. They had been so fascinated by all the birds.

Residents in Poás area

Two young sisters were selling candies at Volcán Poás National Park and were buried alive in a landslide. The police and neighbors found their bodies. A teenage girl died also died near Poás. Her home was on the side of the volcano and was engulfed by a landslide.

Fourteen People in the Restaurant

Less than one mile before we encountered the quake, we passed the La Estrella restaurant in Cinchona. Had we seen it we would have stopped to buy a meal. Only divine intervention kept our eyes from noticing this place.

A few minutes later the restaurant and all fourteen people that were inside disappeared in a landslide. The building was completely demolished. Fourteen people were hurled into eternity, with no warning that death was near.

There could have been twenty-one people in the restaurant, twenty-one people hurled into eternity. Suppose we see the restaurant and decide to stop. Seven boys enter the restaurant and select seats. They look over the drink menu, chatting and smiling. Suddenly the building shakes violently. Earthquake! Chairs screech and tables are shoved as everyone in the building rushes toward the exit door. They cannot get out quickly enough.

An avalanche of dirt rips the restaurant from its foundation. The walls collapse. The roof crashes. The building and its twenty-one occupants slide to the gully below in a terrifying jumble. The victims try to breath but there is no oxygen. Everything goes black. Death is near. Imagine the grief of our family and friends if our bodies were never found.

Missing Family Members

Some people did not know where their friends or family were. Some knew that members of their family were missing, but were they dead or alive? As the hours wore on, the suspense of not knowing became nearly unbearable.

There were people watching the helicopters land at Cariblanco and San Miguel waiting and hoping. Would the next helicopter bring their loved one? Time and again helicopters came and went, bringing in more and more stranded people but their loved ones were not among them.

We saw body bags being unloaded from a helicopter. For those who lost loved ones, they will be among the fortunate ones if the bodies of their loved one will be found. Some bodies were buried so deep under the landslides that they would never be found. How terrible to know that a person you loved had been buried alive and no trace would ever found. It would ease the pain if the body could be found. There probably were many funerals in which there was no casket.

One man who trekked through debris of collapsed houses and damaged roads said, "We passed places where cars were buried, and it stank of bodies." How gruesome!

The White thing in the Landslide

Approximate a mile behind us a white thing could be seen part way down the landslide. That white thing was actually a vehicle. Some of the church brethren went to search out the mysterious sight. Investigation was made to see if someone was in the vehicle.

After digging away some dirt, they uncovered the hand of a person. But, alas, the hand was cold and stiff. Life had fled. I do not know who the person was or whether he was right with God.

Five Chicken Trucks

Among many vehicles that were swept away by landslides, there were five straight trucks, which hauled chicken crates. There were missing in the very area where we were. They slid down one of those steep ravines and vanished. What happened to the truck drivers? If the trucks were missing, I do not see how the drivers survived.

Chapter Twenty

Spiritual Lessons from the Earthquake

I would hardly wish to be caught in such a traumatic situation again, but I thank God for giving us this earthquake experience. It was a time of spiritual growth. Many Scripture passages have more meaning than they ever did before. We will now look at different lessons we learned.

1. *"See the salvation of the Lord."*

After the quake, the road both ahead of us and behind us was destroyed. There was no way to drive or walk out to safety. We were trapped! Usually when we are in trouble, we can receive help from someone, somewhere. But on that day, all our means and efforts were of little value.

A similar thing happened when the Israelites had

just left Egypt. The Red Sea was in front of them and the Egyptians were in pursuit behind them. How could they escape? At first they murmured against Moses and God. But Moses their leader reminded them of the true source of help. "And Moses said unto the people, Fear ye not, stand still, and see the salvation of the Lord" (Exodus 14:13). I like how Moses responded. This was God's message to the children of Israel and it still fits many situations in our day.

While we sat on the hill of El Angel, God seemed to be telling us, "Fear ye not, stand still, and see the salvation of the Lord." He did not want us to become apprehensive of our uncertain situation. He wanted us to simply trust Him, even if we had no idea how or when we would get out. We knew God could work miracles as great as parting the Red Sea.

2. *"Come unto Me, and I will give you rest."*

From the first instant that our SUV was shaking, we felt so helpless. In the days that followed, this helpless feeling hit us many times. Things had gone totally out of our control. Our carefully planned trip was ending up like this! It taught us a greater dependence on God.

When life is going well, we can easily forget to depend on God like we should. When life brings us to a dead end street, we recognize how little we are in control. Our natural impulse struggles within, determined to do something of its own strength. We do not want to wait. We may get a claustrophobic, boxed-in feeling. Still all we can do is wait, wait, and keep waiting.

God has the solution for the problem. "Come unto me, all ye that labor and are heavy laden, and I will give you rest" (Matthew 11:28). He invites us to come, to come as we are. He wants us to drop our own ambitions. He wants us to commit everything to Him. Then He provides rest and security.

We sensed the reality of this promise many times. Despite the rearranged plans and many unsettling moments, we were given an underlying sense of rest. Our Heavenly Father was still in control. The Lord was very near to us.

3. *"Though the mountains shake..."*

Various Scriptures that describe a shaking earth have taken a greater meaning to me. We actually experienced the incredible sensation of Job 9:6, "Which shaketh the earth out of her place, and the pillars thereof tremble."

Psalm 46:1-3 says, "God is our refuge and strength, a very present help in trouble. Therefore will not we fear, though the earth be removed, and though the mountains be carried into the midst of the sea; Though the waters thereof roar and be troubled, though the mountains shake with the swelling thereof. Selah."

Even though the mountains shake, the Almighty God is our refuge and strength. He will take care of us. There is no situation so out of control that we cannot find a refuge in Him. The best thing to do is commit our situation to the One who created the world with His spoken Word.

It is hard to describe the tremendous power of rippling earth and swift landslides. Yet at the same time God cares for each one of his people. He sees each sparrow that falls. What a mighty God!

4. *"I do set my bow in the cloud ...for a covenant."*

During the time we were stranded, we saw four different rainbows. We did not see any later on, as our trip continued. These beautiful colors in the sky were a tremendous encouragement to us while we waited for rescue.

Two of the rainbows formed complete half circles. On one of the half circle rainbows, we saw part of the second rainbow above it. It was quite an awesome sight. It was the first time I ever saw that.

Not only are rainbows a lovely part of God's creation, but they remind us of God's promises to mankind. The rainbow is a special sign of the promise God made to Noah. He would never again destroy the earth with the flood. "I do set my bow in the cloud, and it shall be for a token of a covenant between me and the earth." (Genesis 9:13).

God made many other promises in Scripture. He will not leave us comfortless. He will never leave us nor forsake us. He will be a fortress and a strong tower. He will be our Father and we can be His sons and daughters. He will reward His faithful children with the gift of eternal life.

As we gazed at the rainbows, we clung to the reassurance that God keeps His promises. Again and again He showed His faithfulness. Just as the very first helicopter arrived to pick up the wounded, a beautiful rainbow appeared in the sky. This timing was an overwhelming confirmation that God fulfills His promises.

5. *"His ears are open unto their prayers."*

Shortly after Jeremy called home and talked with his dad, a prayer chain was started. It brought tears to my eyes to think that fellow Christians were taking time to pray for us. Even though we were many miles away from home, we could sense the prayers of the brethren.

This avenue of prayer is a tremendous blessing. The

barriers of distance and language cannot hinder it. Fellow believers from all over the earth can meet at the same mercy seat. "For the eyes of the Lord are over the righteous, and his ears are open unto their prayers: but the face of the Lord is against them that do evil" (1 Peter 3:12).

"The effectual fervent prayer of a righteous man availeth much" (James 5:16). We felt the presence of God in a very real way because of the many people interceding for us.

While we were stranded, there were different times of prayer that were very meaningful and special. Both English and Spanish prayers rose from the hill of El Angel. There were prayers of both gratitude and repentance.

6. *"Take ye heed... for ye know not when the time is."*

One of the most vivid lessons of this earthquake experience was its total surprise. There was no warning. Some other natural events like a tornado can be seen in the distance and the sky grows darker. But an earthquake happens suddenly and unexpectedly.

In the same way, we do not know when our time on earth will be done. God may call us home in the twinkling of an eye. Jesus will return at an hour which no one knows.

It is not so important to know when Jesus will come again or when my life will end. The important thing is to be ready to meet God at all times. "Take ye heed, watch and pray: for ye know not when the time is" (Mark 13:33).

Suppose at the time of the earthquake, I would have had sin in my life. Suppose I would have perished in a landslide. I believe I would have felt wretched and wicked. A feeling of horror would have settled upon me, knowing the awful destination of the unrighteous. I would experience burning forever and ever in that awful lake of fire and brimstone where the worm never dies, and the fire is not quenched. Even if I had been a Christian for over ten years, one sin would have barred me from entering heaven. My life of self-denial would have been of no avail if I had harbored sin at some point. How sad it would have been to lose eternal life all because of rebellion and stubbornness!

I am thankful that I did not have this experience. Had it been the Lord's will to take us home on January 8, 2009, I have confidence that I would have heard those blessed words, "Well done good and faithful servant, enter thou unto the joy of thy Lord."

Why are we seven boys still alive and well? Is it just because we were right with God? Absolutely not. God had a reason why He chose to save us. He must still have a work for us to do. Perhaps part of the work that God had for me was to write this story.

Sometimes I yearn to leave this sinful earth behind and dwell in heaven with my Lord. I wish the Lord had taken me home. Yet I want to use the time He has given me and do His work. It is because of God's mercy and longsuffering that He saved me.

A first responder who witnessed numerous accident scenes said, "In some accidents, because of the severity, I wonder how someone could survive. Yet in other accidents only the bumper is scratched, yet life has fled." He has seen God's protection and he has seen those who passed on. What makes the difference? It determines so much whether it is our time to live or die. God is in control.

*How Is It With **Your** Soul?*

A certain song asks this pointed question: "Are you

living right, should you did tonight? Is it well with your soul?" Life is short, and eternity is long. The choices we make in life determine our destiny.

Friend, how is it with your soul? Would you be ready to meet God if you would draw your last breath today? If you would die without a moment's notice, would you be ready? Is your prayer life active? Is there no unconfessed sin hidden in your heart?

All of us want to go to heaven. That desire is right and good. However, this desire must motivate us to live a pure and holy Christian life or we will miss the mark. Life is too short to harbor sin in one's life. Life is too short to take any chances.

Ask God to help you. "Search me, O God, and know my heart: try me, and know my thoughts. And see if there be any wicked way in me, and lead me in the way everlasting" (Psalm 139:23-24).

Sometimes it is easy to forget why we are put on the earth. We are here to bring honor and glory to God, not to build a physical empire. Our earthquake experiences have reaffirmed that if a person stares death in the eye, many of the physical things that once seemed so important seem like vanity. What are we doing that will last when the world is on fire? Ask yourself, "Am I building things of eternal or earthly value?"

Our job should be to do things for the Lord, but our day-to-day work should be to pay the expenses. However, our true goal is eternal. This is what God wants of each of His children. Let us live today as if we would die tomorrow. Then we are ready to start living.

God is Good

My God is good, oh yes He's good
I trust Him for He knows the way,
He knows my path though dark unknown,
I want to in His bosom stay.

My God is good, Christ died for me,
My sin so great my thoughts were vain.
I needed one to pardon me,
The blood of Jesus I will claim.

My God is good, my sin is gone,
Great was the debt that I did owe.
Forgiven now I'm free at last,
I'll serve my God and Him alone.

My God is good, He is my God,
I stand in awe that I'm His child.
Though vile and sinful tho' I was,
He gladly claims me as His child.

My God is good, He is my friend,
My life is yours I'm in your hand.
Committed to You I will be,
I'll meet you in the Glory land.

Written by: Samuel Beachy
December 2008
This poem was written 2-3 weeks before the earthquake.

Epilogue

August 2009 -

Since our earthquake experience in Costa Rica, some changes worth mentioning are as follows.

My family, the Marvin Beachys moved from Belvidere, Tennessee to Fredonia, Kentucky in April 2009. This is part of an outreach effort from the Belvidere Mennonite Church. Here I am engaged in a lawn care business.

Lewis Stutzman married Malinda Lehman in April of 2009. Presently they live in Brown County, Ohio. He delivers storage barns for a living.

Jeremy Weaver is planning to get married to Jennifer Miller on September 19, 2009.